REMINISCENCES *of* COLONEL HENRY ERNST DOSCH

This booklet, the thirty-fourth to come from Ye Galleon Press, is No. 2535 in Smith's Pacific Northwest Americana, where it is alphabetized under Dosch rather than Lockley, presumably the author. Sheets for five-hundred copies were printed and from these two hundred paper bound booklets were made in late August, 1972, with the remaining sheets held in reserve.

Of this edition 200 *copies were printed.*

This is Copy No. 167 .

REMINISCENCES

OF

COL. HENRY ERNST DOSCH

BY

FRED LOCKLEY

YE GALLEON PRESS
FAIRFIELD, WASHINGTON
1972

ISBN 0-87770-081-8

REMINISCENCES OF COLONEL HENRY ERNST DOSCH

By Fred Lockley

Colonel Henry Ernst Dosch is one of Oregon's most useful citizens. I spent several recent afternoons with Colonel Dosch and the more I talked to him, the more I was impresed with the versatility of his knowledge. He is not only an authority on horticulture, but he has a profound knowledge of history, literature and of the traditions of the Old West, of which he was a part.

"I was born at Meinz-on-the-Rhine, June 17, 1841," said Colonel Dosch. "My father's name was John Baptiste Dosch. My mother's maiden name was Anna Busch. There were seven children in our family, of whom I am the eldest. I was named Ernst after my father's brother, Colonel Ernst Dosch, who was Colonel of the Hungarian Blue Hussars. Another brother of my father's, my uncle Anton, was Colonel of the Red Hussars. My uncle was a government official in the Customs Department. My father was a classmate with Bismarck, which later proved to be a most fortunate thing for him, for in 1848, during the German Revolution my father organized a regiment to resist the Prussians. When the revolution was ruthlessly suppressed by the Prussians, the revolutionists had to run for their live—some went to Switzerland, while a great many emigrated to the United States. My father, on account of having been a classmate of Bismarck's, was allowed to stay in Germany. Many of the revolutionists, the best blood of Germany, came to the United States and settled at Belleville, 20 miles east of St. Louis. During the Civil War there were at least 10,000 German turners from St. Louis, Belleville and the country thereabouts, who enlisted in the Union Army and gave a good account of themselves, as they kept Missouri in the Union.

"I came to America in 1860, when I was between 18

and 19 years of age. My father was well-to-do, so when I was a boy I had a private tutor. Later I went to the Colege of Commerce and Industry for four years. I graduated from the engineering department. At that time it was the custom to pay for apprenticeships, so my father paid for an apprenticeship for me in a commercial house. The honor men in the schools and colleges were compelled to serve but one year instead of three in the Grman Army. As I was an honor man, I was only required to put in one year of service. I wanted to come to the United States, but on account of the requirements for military service, I could not leave unless I could pass the examination for reserve officer. I passed this examination successfully and secured a passport which entitled me to be absent for one year, after which I was required to come back and serve in the German Army. I had not been in the United States long till the Civil War broke out and I at once enlisted in Fremont's bodyguard. In the early days of the Civil War, the military service was honeycombed by political intrigue and favoritism. An intrigue was formed against Fremont, and General Hunter was sent to relieve him. This was just on the eve of an attack on the Confederate General Price. Price in the mix-up escaped, and Hunter was superseded. Fremont's bodyguard were discharged after our fight at Springfield, October 25, 1861, in which I was wounded, and I went to St. Louis and re-enlisted in the 5th Missouri Cavalry. Captain Nathaniel Lyon, a loyal and able officer was in command of the St. Louis Arsenal. St. Louis was full of Southern sympathizers. The Confederates were seizing arms, ordnance and supplies wherever they were located in the South, and as the governor of Missouri favored the secessionists had it not been for the energetic action of Captain Lyon, the arsenal at St. Louis would have fallen into the hands of southern sympathizers. Governor Jackson ordered the militia into camp in the vicinity of the arsenal. These men were armed with guns sent up from Baton Rouge. Many of the militiamen wore badges of the Confederate Army. Captain Lyon, learning that they were going to try to seize the arsenal, surrounded the militia and demanded their surrender. The next day after the surrender of the state troops, Captain Harney arrived in St. Louis and assumed command. Shortly after this Captain Harney became Brigadier General of the First Brigade of Missouri Volunteers. Among the officers who distinguished themselves in the operations in Missouri at this time were Colonel Siegel and Colonel Osterhaus. After the bloody battle of Wilson's Creek in which General Nathaniel Lyon was killed, I was ordered to take a squad of men there to bring back his body. We served as the honor guard. Before long I became Sergeant-Major and was acting adjutant of the regiment. When our Colonel resigned, I commanded the regiment. After receiving my honorable discharge at the end of my enlistment, a comrade of mine, Fred Keisel, told me that there was a freight train at Omaha, belonging to Kimball and Lawrence, loading supplies to take to Salt Lake City. Henry Lawrence wanted a book-keeper and also a drygoods clerk for his store in Salt Lake City. I was engaged as the book-keeper and Fred as the clerk. When we got to Omaha we found that the wagon boss was short of drivers. He offered Fred and me $20 apiece if we would serve as bullwhackers and drive four yoke of oxen. We accepted the job. At that time Omaha had about 40 buildings, my recollection now being that most of them were saloons, livery stables or blacksmith shops. I will never forget our trip across the plains. About 100 miles out of Omaha we came across a store kept by a half-breed French-Canadian. For the next 400 miles there was no settlement of any kind. The prairie, covered with wild flowers, stretched unbroken in all directions to the far horizon. In all directions we could see countless herds of antelopes, while at times the buffalo seemed to blacken the rolling land waves in the distance. Prairie chickens and sage hens were abundant. We were 58 days making the trip to Salt Lake City. We reached there in the summer of 1863. Fred settled in Salt Lake City, became a state senator, built up a large business in Salt Lake City and Sacramento and became wealthy. Salt Lake City did not appeal to me, so with six other young men, I decided to go on to California. We bought a wagon and a yoke of oxen and headed westward.

"On the way out from Omaha, near Laramie, we met Jim Bridger, a very likeable and reliable man. I also met Bill Hutchison and Bill Hickman. Bill Hickman is the author of a book in which he tells his experiences while serving as one of Brigham Young's 'destroying angels.' He was a fanatic, and being quite ignorant, he believed anything and everything that Brigham Young told him. Just ahead of us there was a wagon train which was traveling fast. We were rapidly overtaking them but we never saw them, that is, alive. At the head of the Humboldt Divide, we found where the members of this party had dug trenches to resist attack. The horses, women and girls had all ben taken, the men had been killed and we found their bodies lying beside the burned wagons. The massacre had evidently occurred a couple of days before, and all that was left to tell the tale was a lot of wagon tires, thimble skeins and chains and mutilated bodies. Three days before this massacre 300 Indians in war paint had overtaken us, stopped us and looked through our wagon and then gone on. Evidently they were after the wagon train ahead, which they overtook and destroyed.

"When on my trip westward from Salt Lake City, I got to Virginia City, I landed a job at road building, and some time later I became a Wells-Fargo express rider.

"Probably there never was a town which was more wide open than Virginia City," said Colonel Dosch. "The saloon men, barkeepers and gamblers were the aristocrats of the community, and their vassals were blacklegs, road agents and thugs. When I struck Virginia City, my money had about run out, so I took the first job that offered, which was a pick-and-shovel job. They were building a road over the Pass and I was put on as one of the worknem. Having graduated from an engineering course in a technical school in Germany, I showed the foreman how to lay out the road so we could go over the hill on an easy grade. Pretty soon the supervisor came along and asked who had laid out that road. The foreman pointed me out, so Mr. Moore came to me, and when he found out that I was a college man he said, 'We can find plenty of men to do pick-and-shovel work. You should have a better job than this. If you were only a good rider I could get you a job on the pony express.' I told him I had served in the cavalry so I could qualify as a rider. He told me to report to the Wells-Fargo Company in Virginia City to take the run from Virginia City to Friday Station on Lake Bigler, as Lake Tahoe was then called. I rode from Virginia City to Gold Hill, Silver City, Pioneer and to Carson, where I changed horses. Then to a Mormon station and over the hill to Friday Station. I changed horses three times on this thirty-three mile run and was required to make the run in three hours. I carried letters only, for which the Wells-Fargo Company received 25 cents each. The regular stage left at 7:00 A. M. for Placerville. We left at 4:00 P. M., overtaking the stage at Placerville. A narrow gauge railroad ran from Placerville to Sacramento. By using the pony express the business men gained one day in time, thus speeding up their correspondence. I became well acquainted with Samuel Clemens, better known to the general public as Mark Twain, who was a reporter on the Virginia City Enterprise at that time. He was a likeable chap. He used to come around and say, 'What do you know in the way of news today? Anything exciting happen on the run today?' Once in a while I would have a good item of news for him, though as far as that goes, there was no shortage of news in Virginia City, as they had a man for breakfast almost every morning. One night as I was making my run, my horse shied out to one side and would not pass a clump of several juniper trees along the road. I finally forced him back into the road and then I discovered why the horse had shied. From each of these small trees was suspended a man with a rope around his neck, and on each of their chests was pinned a notice from the Vigilance Committee. You should have seen the clearing out of Virginia City after that lynching bee. At another time as one of the saloon men in Virginia City came to his door to see me start out on my run, a man stepped out and shot the saloonkeeper through the heart. Instantly the barkeeper shot the murderer, who also fell fatally wounded, but before he cashed in his checks, he shot the barkeeper and also killed him, so inside of sixty seconds there were three dead men. The alkali dust on my run from Virginia City to Friday Station was so bad that I began bleeding from my lungs, so I had to give up the run. I went to Sacramento and took passage on the *Cosmopolitan* for San Francisco. This boat, the *Cosmopolitan,* is now at Seattle and is used as the *Bluebird* is here, for dancing. I tried to land a job at San Francisco, but jobs seemed hard to land. For three days I slept on the wharf and lived on crackers and cheese. Finally I became desperate and decided to enlist on the frigate *Saranac,* which was in the bay and which had a recruiting office in the city. I passed the recruiting office at least a score of times and every time I stopped to go in I would shy off and think, 'Maybe something will turn up,' and sure enough when I had just about reached the end of my string, I ran across Henry Garth who had come across the plains with me. Henry didn't have much more money than I had, which was none at all, but he had an uncle at Petaluma. He suggested that we go to Petaluma, as he knew his uncle would give us both a job. We made our way there and Henry asked his uncle for a job for us both. Henry's uncle threw him out bodily and told him to beat it, so we had our walk for nothing. I went to the hotel and told the proprietor I was broke and wanted to stay with him and would pay as soon as I got a job. He told me that he could get me a job and that I could board at his hotel. He sent me to the manager of a match factory there, which manufactured these old-fashioned sulphur matches, you remember the kind—there were 100 of them in a block. The manager gave me a job and told me to report for work next morning. That night I was awakened by a lot of excitement, and getting up I found there was a big fire. I dressed hurriedly and when I got out on the street, I was told that the match factory was on fire. It was a total loss and I was out of a job. I went down to the wharf where I found a sloop called the *Harriet Lane* was about to sail for San Francisco. I asked the captain for a chance to work my way to San Francisco. He said that he was loaded with potatoes and that I could go to San Francisco with him and that he would give me a job unloading the potatoes and pay me for it, so I got aboard. When we reached San Francisco an officer was waiting for the boat and attached it for debt, so tht job went glimmering. I began to think I never would be able to get work. I began a systematic campaign for a job and finally landed a job with a pick and shovel on the site now occupied by the Palace Hotel. We were paid $1 a day for ten hours work. A Chinaman brought us our lunch in a big pan, which we set on the sidewalk and each man dipped in and helped himself. The sand we were shoveling away was loaded on cars and hauled off to make a fill. A rather interesting thing in connection with my job here was that the engine used in hauling the sand away that I was shoveling onto the cars, was later sent to be used as the first engine on the portage road at the Cascades. It was a small engine and the rails used on the portage road were wooden rails with iron straps. When the Lewis & Clark Exposition was held here in Portland I met Mr. Hughes. He introduced me to Mr. Elliott, who had been the engineer when I was working for $1 a day in San Francisco. He was a brother-in-law of Leland Stanford. The little engine used at the Cascades had been shipped back to San Francisco as a historic souvenir of the early days of San Francisco. I told him that we would like to have this engine exhibited at the Lewis & Clark Fair, as it was the first engine used in Oregon. He fixed it up in fine shape, gave it to me with his compliments and paid the freight on it to Portland. You probably remember seeing it standing beside the 120-ton engine of the Union Pacific at the Lewis & Clark Fair. As it was my personal property, I turned it over to the Oregon Historical Society when the Lewis & Clark Exposition closed and I understand that it was allowed to go to rack and ruin. It is too bad, as it should have been preserved because of its historical interest. After working ten days at this job in San Francisco at $1 a day, I couldn't stand the hotel off any longer, so I applied for my money. I was told that they paid off at the end of the month and not before, and that if a person didn't work a month they received no pay, so I quit then and there. I met an old-time acquaintance named Bendel of the firm of Tilman & Bendel, wholesale grocery merchants, who nearly laughed himself sick when he saw me, for my clothes were pretty well shot to pieces. He handed me $20 and told me to come around to his store. The merchants at that time had an agreement not to employ men who had not been passed upon by the secretary of the employment association. I invested my $20 in clothes and went up to see the secretary. He talked with me a few minutes and offered me my choice of seven different positions. It was a case of 'it never rains but it pours.' Here I had been running my legs off for a job without being able to land one and now I could have my choice of jobs. He told me that A. Cohn & Company were operating seven stores and he advised me to accept a position with them. H. F. Bloch was the head of the firm. He put me to work making out bills. Their store in San Francisco was known as A. Cohn & Company. They also operated one in Portland under the same name on the corner of Pine and Front streets. Their store in The Dalles was Known as Bloch,Miller & Company. They operated one in Walla Walla under the name of Schwabacher Brothers and the name of their Boise store was Schwabacher Brothers & Frank. They also had a store in Placerville and one in Colville. Mr. Bloch, after trying me out for a short time, told me to report to Bloch, Miller & Company at The Dalles. At that time there were two steamers a month plying between San Francisco and Portland. I came on the *Panama,* of which Captain Connor was the master. It took us seven days to make the trip. At that time there was only 15 feet of water on the Columbia Bar and as the *Panama* was fairly heavily loaded, it bumped on the bar three times in crossing. I landed at Portland on Sunday, April 9, 1864, getting off at the Allen & Lewis wharf at C street. I stopped that night at the New York Hotel. Their rooms were 25 cents a day. In those days it was well known up and down the coast as the 'two-bit' house. Next morning at 5:00 A. M. I took the boat for The Dalles, of which Captain John R. Wolf was master. In 1864, when I started to work for Bloch, Miller & Company, they had the only stone building in Oregon and also the largest store in the state. We handled general merchandise and miners' supplies and we also operated a warehouse for transferring goods by pack train to the mines. The Dalles had a population at that time of not less than 2,700, and it was always thronged with transients on their way to and from the mines. There was more life in The Dalles in a day than there was in Portland in a month. I was put in charge of buying the gold dust. This doesn't sound as if it would be a very responsible job, but it was, for it wasn't merely a matter of weighing out the dust—it was a matter of deciding how much we could pay for it and make a reasonable profit. Gold dust from districts where there was silver in which the gold dust had a certain alloy of silver was worth $10 an ounce, while the gold dust from Canyon City or Florence was worth $17 an ounce. If the gold dust came from a district where there was copper, it had a different color and commanded a lower price. I averaged to buy $50,000 worth of gold dust a month, which was sent direct to the mint in San Francisco. Most of the saloons and merchants at The Dalles accepted gold dust in payment for their wares and sold the dust to us. In those days The Dalles was a wide open town. It was never a tough town like Virginia City. George Clayton ran the biggest gambling house in eastern Oregon there. You could get action on your money through poker, faro, three-card-monte, or you could bet your money on the small horses. Cigars were fifty cents and drinks two-bits. In fact, a quarter was the smallest coin used. Mary St. Clair, who was known from British Columbia to Old Mexico, was one of the famous characters of The Dalles in those days. She would charge you $20 a bottle for champagne, but she would hand the money over to anyone who needed it just as cheerfully as she took it. She had a heart as big as an ox, and if anyone was sick, she was the first one to offer help and the last one to leave. Vic Trevitt ran the Mt. Hood saloon just across from Mary St. Clair's place. Vic really ran a sort of gentleman's club. He wouldn't allow a drunken man in the place, neither would he allow gambling. He wouldn't stand for a rough house nor rough talk. In fact, you saw very few drunken men in The Dalles in those days. Everyone went heeled, so there was very little fighting, for in case of trouble it was a case of who was quickest on the trigger. It made people a little cautious about starting anything. So much gold dust was coming in that the citizens started an agitation for a mint, and in 1865 Congress appropriated $100,000 and a contract was let for the building of the mint. The rock was brought from Mill Creek, about five miles from The Dalles. After the first story was completed, Congress decided that the mint at San Francisco was sufficient and sold the site and the building for a song. In 1864 The Dalles was the trading center for a large part of Idaho, Montana, and eastern Washington. Merchants came from Boise, Walla Walla, Missoula and many other points to secure their supplies from the merchants of The Dalles. While The Dalles had a permanent population at that time of over 2,500, its floating population frequently was two or three times that number. Among the well-known men in The Dalles in that day were Joseph Wilson, Z. F. Moody, Judge Humason, Judge Gates, Judge D. D. Hidden, Dr. Shackleford, Dr. Bryan, Dr. Hoffman, Frank Dodge, agent of the O. S. N. Co., Nick Sinnott, who with Hanley kept the Umatilla House, and by the way, the Umatilla House in those days was a regular mint. They took in more money over their bar than all the other hotel in The Dalles put together. Those were the days when the Oregon Steam Navigation Company also made money hand-over-fist. They charged $60 a ton on freight from Portland to The Dalles. Fare was $20 and meals were $1.00. The boats were always crowded to capacity with passengers, so that meals were being served continuously, and, of course, the bar on the boat was busy all day long. They don't serve meals anymore, such as were served in those days. They used to serve ham and eggs, tenderloin steak, fried potatoes, venison, hot cakes and coffee for breakfast. The Oregon Steam Navigation Company had a monopoly on the Columbia River. Frequently a steamer would make from $3,000 to $5,000 on a single trip. The record profit was made on May 13, 1862, when one boat made a profit of over $10,000. The principal stockholders of the Oregon Steam Navigation Company were W. S. Ladd, R. R. Thompson, Simeon G. Reed, Jacob Kamm, J. C. Ainsworth, B. F. Bradford, L. W. Coe, Benjamin Stark, Richard Williams, George W. Hoyt, Josiah Myrick, and some others. Captain John H. Wolf, with whom I made my first trip to The Dalles, was one of the best-known mariners on the Columbia River run. In the middle sixties he was in command of the *New World*. Among the well-known steamers of the day were the *Wilson G. Hunt*, the *Carrie Ladd*, the *Express* and the *Cascades*. The *New World* ran from Portland to the Cascades and the *Hassalo* from the Cascades to the Dalles. After putting in a year at The Dalles, I went to Canyon City. This was in 1865. I went into partnership with John Snively, who ran a pack train, and William Claflin. My partners furnished the capital and I furnished the experience. We carried a $25,000 stock and we complied with the universal custom of those days of selling our goods at double what they cost us. This rule did not hold good in the case of flour, for we sold flour sometimes as low as 55 cents a pound, and when you know that the freight from The Dalles to Canyon City was 55 cents a pound, you will realize that we sold it for the cost of transportation and were out the orignial cost of the flour. However, we made up the loss on other things. When I went there Grant County had recently been organized. Canyon City was largely settled by the left wing of Price's army. They had left Missouri and most of them had been southern sympathizers. W. Lair Hill was county judge and Tom Brents was county clerk. At the next election Mike Goodwin, a saloonkeeper, was elected county clerk, and as he knew nothing about the duties and could not afford to neglect his saloon, he made me his deputy. C. H. Miller had been elected county judge. He had been an express messenger, a miner, had tried his hand at running a newspaper, had lived with the Indians, and when I knew him first, he was a devoted admirer of Byron. He tried to imitate Byron in every way, even to limping like Byron. I was his unwilling victim. He was constantly writing poetry and coming into my office to read it to me. He was a picturesque character for he wore his hair long and wore high boots, tucking the trousers in one boot and letting the other trouser leg cover the boot. He was really a pretty able lawyer and a very genial man, but I wasn't very crazy about his poetry. He sent his verses to the Times-Mountaineer at The Dalles, publishing it under the name of John Smith, Jr. Later he ran a good deal of his verse in the Blue Mountain Eagle at Canyon City under his own name of C. H. Miller. Still later he adopted the name of Joaquin Miller, and when he went to England, his picturesque attire and his western manners made a big hit. His wife, Minnie Myrtle Miller, to my mind, was a better poet than her husband, but her verse has never been published except in newspaper form.

"On July 10, 1866, I was married to Marie Louise Fleurot, who was born in France and who came to Portland in 1857. She attended St. Mary's Academy in Portland for eight years. Her father and mother ran the French Hotel at Canyon City. This hotel was next to my store and there I became acquainted with my future wife. We were married by Father Macklin, a fine, bighearted Irish priest. After having been in Canyon City for about five years, one August day—and it was 104 in the shade—one of the buildings caught fire. Canyon City, as its names indicates, is in a canyon, and the flames swept from building to building and within a short time the city was like a roaring furnace. Two hundred and fifty five buildings were reduced to ashes, among them our store. In 1870, when I was burned out at Canyon City, I came to Portland. Having had no insurance on my store or stock of goods, I was broke and had to get something to do. At that time Judge Otto Kramer's father ran a store here. He gave me a job as porter and janitor at $40 a month. After a while I was promoted to salesman at $75 a month, and later my salary was raised to $100 a month. When Mr. Kramer sold out I became head book-keeper at $150 a month. Still later I became manager of the store at $300 a month. Eventually I became one of the partners of the firm with Ben Selling and Frank Aiken. We sold out ni 1890. For 21 years I had worked steadily without taking a vacation and my health had become greatly impaired. I bought the ranch on which I now live, and drinking the water from the iron spring here and working outdoors restored my health completely. I had always been fond of nature and so took up horticulture as a hobby. I sent to France, Germany, England and to various other places for walnuts, as I believed that the Willamette Valley was adapted to growing walnuts, although all my friends thought I was crazy. I bought 17 acres here at Dosch Station on Dosch Road 36 years ago. It is part of the old Clinton-Kelly donation land claim. When I was a boy in Germany the students of our school made two walking trips a year, spending a week at a time studying botany, horticulture and forestry. We stopped overnight at farmhouses or slept in barns. When I came to my place here, I remembered how greatly I had enjoyed studying horticulture and botany as a boy, so I began experimenting along horticultural lines. I made my vegetable garden support my family while I experimented with various fruits and nuts. I discovered that the reason that English walnuts had not done well in Oregon was that the right variety had not been brought here—that in many cases the male walnut blossom had bloomed and the bloom had dropped off before the female walnut flower blossomed. For 15 years I worked away at developing best types of walnut trees for the Willamette Valley and finally introduced the Franquette and Mayette walnuts. Then I began talking walnut growing. Charlie Ladd put out a lot of walnuts and so did Mr. Prince at Dundee. Then the McGill and McDonald nursery commercialized it and introduced them widely. Today California is sending to Oregon to secure Franquette walnut trees. From the few acres I planted for experimental purposes, the industry has grown until we now have 14,000 acres here in the Willamette Valley set to walnuts. No I didn't make any money on it—in fact, I didn't expect to make money. I did it for the love of it and to introduce a new industry to Oregon. I helped organize the Oregon Horticultural Society 40 years ago. Dr. J. A. Cardwell, an enthusiastic horticulturist, became the first president of the society and continued as president for 20 years. E. R. Lake, now of Washington, D. C., was the first secretary. I am the sole surviving member of the State Horticultural Society of Oregon, organized 20 years ago. I am also the only member of the State Board of Horticulture appointed 34 years ago by Governor Pennoyer. I am now serving my fourth term as secretary of the State Board of Horticulture. My first term was served as successor to George Lambertson. I next succeeded John Minto. H. M. Williamson was then elected and served for 11 years. In 1888 I served as post commander of Garfield Post G. A. R. This post was organized 42 years ago and there are only three of the 36 charter members now living. Judge J. H. Northrup, H. F. Lamb and myself.

Prior to the World's Fair in Chicago I went to Salem and secured the passage of a law authorizing the appointment of a commission to represent Oregon at the World's Fair. Governor Pennoyer had no use for commissions. He told me that he would appoint a commissioner, but that I would have to serve alone and he could thus place responsibility. When the legislature passed the law which I had urged, Governor Pennoyer vetoed it. Once more I went to the bat with the legislators and the bill was passed over his veto, and I was authorized to name the commissioners. One of the first men I named was Dr. J. A. Cardwell, for no one in Oregon was more entitled to a place on the commission than Dr. Cardwell. Oregon took sweepstakes for the entire United States on grain. Look up the records of the World's Fair and you will find that we took 17 gold medals, receiving the highest awards along many lines. I handled Oregon's exhibit at the Omaha Exposition. Not only did I receive no salary for this work, but it cost me $1,200 of my own money, but I was glad to contribute not only my time but my money towards advancing Oregon's interests.

While at Omaha some railroad men were attracted to Oregon's exhibit of timber. Later they bought timber from Oregon to build 20 miles of trestles. Some boat builders, who operated on the Susquehanna River, were also greatly attracted by our timber exhibit and they later sent to Oregon and bought lumber for the building of 200 river barges. We also made a very decided impression on eastern markets with our shingles and dried prunes.

From Omaha I went to Buffalo in 1900, and if you will look up the records of that exposition you will find that no other state took as many prizes as Oregon.

The next place where I was installed and was in charge of Oregon's exhibit was at Charleston, South Carolina. We had here a timber 74 feet long and 3 feet square which came from the Eastern & Western Lumber Company's mills. Originally it had been 115 feet long and 3 feet square, but they had to cut it down to 74 feet to get it through a tunnel which was built on a curve in Montana. I also had there a timber 20 feet long and 9 feet in diameter. This had 365 rings, showing it was 365 years old. A prominent official of the German government thought these two big timbers had been specially prepared and he tried his best to see where they were joined together. He couldn't believe it possible that we grew timbers of this size. I told him that he could place an order for a thousand such sticks and the Portland mills would fill his order. I gave him a letter to a Portland lumberman. He came out to Portland, discovered that I had been teling the truth, and purchased a cargo of bridge timbers. He has been back to Portland several times since and has been one of our best customers.

In 1903 I went to Japan to see if I could persuade

Japan to make an exhibit at the Lewis & Clark Fair. They had appropriated $800,000 for an exhibit at St. Louis and I wanted them to appropriate a further sum of $200,000 to bring their exhibit to Portland. I found that it would be hopeless to have the measure passed by the Japanese Diet. The only thing left to do was to use a little diplomacy. I had a warm friend and advocate in one of the Japanese officials, and succeeded in securing the appropriation.

As an indication of their appreciation of my work, I had conferred upon me the Order of the Sacred Treasure which is a military decoration and at that time very few had been bestowed upon foreigners.

In 1903, while in Japan, I met Baron Chinda and Baron Komura. They told me of the trouble they were having from Beri-Beri.. The Japanese soldiers and peasants were eating rice from Cochin-China. This rice cost two and three-fourths cents a pound. I said, 'Why do you not buy Louisiana rice? You can get it at the same price and your soldiers and citizens will not get Beri-Beri from it.' Possibly a year after that I was sent to New Orleans to invite Louisiana to take part in our exposition, and as I went into the St. Charles Hotel I noticed three Japanese sitting in the lobby. As they caught sight of me they rose, bowed low, and one of them said, 'Are you not Colonel Dosch?' Looking at him closely I recognized him and remembered his name, which was Watta Napa. I said 'Yes, my name is Colonel Dosch and you are Watta Napa. You are the chief clerk in Baron Komura's office.' He said 'Do you remember, Colonel Dosch, teling Baron Komura about Louisiana rice?' I had almost forgotten the circumstance. I thought a moment and said, 'Yes, but nothing ever came of it.' He said, 'Oh yes, very much came of it. I have just dispatched a shipload of rice from here and am planning to contract for the entire crop.' As a matter of fact, they did purchase that year's crop of Louisana rice, and the Japanese-

Russian War was fought on Louisiana rice. Not only that but the price of rice advanced from 2¾ cents to 7 cents a pound, so it brought a great deal of prosperity to the planters of Louisiana. The high price of rice also caused the introduction of rice growing into Texas. So you see that no man liveth unto himself alone.

"Once more, I had almsot forgotten the incident when I was notified that I had been given the title of Baron and the Japanese government was bestowing upon me the Decoration of the Rising Sun. The first man to receive this decoration in the United States was President Eliot of Harvard. I was the second one to receive the decoration. Colonel Roosevelt was the third, President Taft the fourth, General Pershing the fifth, and a few months ago it was bestowed upon W. D. Wheelwright, so there are only six men who have had this decoration bestowed upon them in the United States—so I am in good company. The decoration carries with it many immunities and privileges in Japan. At the time I had charge of the Oregon exhibit in Japan I was fortunate in making many warm friends among the Japanese.

"At the Lewis & Clark Fair I was director of exhibits and privileges and was also in charge of the Oregon exhibit at the Alaska-Yukon Pacific Exposition, and I helped prepare and organize the Oregon exhibit for the Panama-Pacific Exposition.

"You asked me a moment or two ago about my children. I have had ten children. Our first child, Marie Louise, was born in Canyon City and died when she was a little girl. Ernest Pierre, my next child, is with a steamship company here in Portland. Lily died eight years ago. John Baptiste and Henry Ernst, our twins, died when they were three years old, of whooping cough. My daughter Camille and my little grandson were killed four years ago at Bertha Station by a collision between two electric trains. Arno was my next boy. The next children were twins, Roswell and Walter. Walter died as a child, and Roswell, who was a sculptor and who was a member of the faculty of the University of Oregon, died not long ago. He was a lieutenant in the World War. Marguerite and her husband, David Campbell, who is head of the censervatory of music, with their two little girls, live with me here in the old home.

"Arno you knew well when you were on the Pacific Monthly. Arno was born here in Portland, attended the Portland academy, then went to law school and read law with Williams, Wood and Linthicum. He was admitted to the bar when he was twenty years old. They tell me he made a brilliant record at the Harvard Law School, graduating there in three years. Returning to Portland he decided that he preferred to be a journalist so he went to work for Harvey Scott and was a reporter on the Oregonian for four years. Later he became editor of the Pacific Monthly. From here he went to San Franicsco and worked for a while on the Bulletin. Later he started a magazine there called "The East and West." From San Francisco he went to New York City. Young Pulitzer and young Page, who liked Arno, were writers, and who were his chums at Harvard, helped him secure a position writing special articles for the Worlds Work. Arno was in Belgium before the Germans invaded it in 1914 and was there and all over Europe during the four years of the war. He also visited Russia, Egypt, Greece, and now is in Germany writing special articles which appear daily in the papers of the United States.

"In 1866 I joined the Order of Odd Fellows and in 1888 I was elected Grand Master of Oregon."